# TRUE
# Prayer

Colin Urquhart

Kingdom Faith Resources Ltd.
Roffey Place, Old Crawley Road,
HORSHAM West Sussex, RH12 4RU
Tel: 01293 851543 Fax: 01293 854610
E-mail: resources@kingdomfaith.com
www.kingdomfaith.com

First published in Great Britain in March 2003 by Kingdom Faith
Kingdom Faith Trust is a registered charity (no.278746)

Copyright © 2003 Colin Urquhart

All rights reserved. No part of this publication may be reproduced, stored in a retrieval system, or transmitted in any form or by any means, electronic, mechanical, photocopying or otherwise, without the prior consent of the publisher. Short extracts may be used for review purposes.

Unless otherwise stated, Scripture taken from the
HOLY BIBLE, NEW INTERNATIONAL VERSION.
Copyright © 1973, 1978, 1984 by International Bible Society.
Used by permission of Hodder and Stoughton Limited.

ISBN 1-900409-45-3

# Acknowledgements

I thank the Lord for a lifetime of prayer, the most wonderful privilege God has given men! That we should be able to relate to Him personally in prayer never ceases to amaze me! And all thanks are really due to Him!

At the human level, I am thankful for all with whom I have shared in prayer corporately over the years: my wife and family, the various community households in which we have lived, the team of Kingdom workers and the Church of which I am a part.

I also acknowledge the devoted work of Mary, David and Cliss in preparing this book. May it encourage you to devote yourself to Jesus in prayer, and be an inspiration that will enrich your prayer life!

Colin Urquhart

# CONTENTS

| | |
|---|---|
| WHAT IS PRAYER? | 7 |
| WHAT DOES JESUS SAY ABOUT PRAYER? | 11 |
| THE LORD'S PRAYER | 15 |
| ASK | 29 |
| FAITH | 33 |
| HEARING FROM GOD | 39 |
| AUTHORITY TO HAVE VICTORY | 43 |
| NO CONDEMNATION | 53 |
| THE NEED OF DISCIPLINE | 57 |
| METHODS | 59 |
| CORPORATE PRAYER | 71 |
| DISTRACTIONS | 75 |
| CONCLUSION | 79 |

# 1

## WHAT IS PRAYER?

Prayer is essentially about relationship with God. There are as many different ways to pray as there are to relate to a person. Some have a deep, loving relationship with God in prayer. Others know the Lord only on the level of an acquaintance. There are those who do not even know the One to whom they speak.

As with any relationship, it takes time to build an intimate relationship with God in prayer. Of course, any relationship involves two-way communication, listening as well as speaking! In prayer, you learn not only how to address God and view the circumstance in which you are placed; you learn also how to hear His voice, to know what He is saying to you as opposed to your own thoughts or ideas.

In this short book we can only look briefly at the most essential principles of prayer. This will be enough either to help you to begin to pray effectively, or to widen your experience in prayer. We will be very practical, for it is knowing *how* to pray that will draw us into a closer relationship with God through Jesus Christ.

Most people feel they are failures when they pray. They feel they never, or hardly ever, break through to God. They wonder whether anyone is listening to them; and even if God does hear, is He going to take any notice of anyone so insignificant? Will anything really happen in response to my prayer? They are discouraged because it seems that when they have prayed, their requests have been refused. They simply feel totally ineffective, and sometimes imagine it to be better not to pray at all, than to feel that God is refusing them.

Understandable though these attitudes are, they are simply the result of not knowing *how* to pray with the assurance that the Lord not only hears but will surely answer. Many have never been taught to pray, only that they should pray, but without receiving the motivation to do so.

I speak as one who has prayed for well over 50 years and spent the last 40 of these teaching others *how* to pray. **I want to show you how *you* can have a rich prayer life by introducing you to different ways of praying showing you how to establish a real relationship with God in prayer, knowing He hears you.**

Of course I cannot do your praying for you. Just as you have to build your relationship with others, so you have to build your own relationship with God in prayer! This short book will show you *how* to do this.

Even if you are used to praying regularly, you will be able to broaden your understanding of prayer and to have your spiritual life enriched by being introduced to different ways of praying.

Prayer does not seem real unless you have a personal relationship with Jesus Christ. Once you are born again and have God's Holy

Spirit living in you, prayer is transformed by the fact that you *know* the One to whom you pray. If you do not know the Lord in this way, I suggest you read *'True Salvation'*, *'True Love'*, or *'True Life'*, for each of these short books will help you come into such a relationship with God the Father through His Son, Jesus.

# 10 • TRUE PRAYER

# 2. WHAT DOES JESUS SAY ABOUT PRAYER?

In the Sermon on the Mount Jesus gives very practical instruction about prayer:

> *"When you pray, go into your room, close the door and pray to your Father, who is unseen. Then your Father, who sees what is done in secret, will reward you." (Matthew 6: 6)*

a) There is a time for praying with others, as we shall see later. However if you are to develop the personal relationship with God that will enrich your life, you need to obey Jesus and do things the way He says. His instructions here are clear. **Go into a room privately on your own, so you can pray out your heart to God and not be distracted or inhibited by the presence of others.**

b) You are coming as a child to the One who loves you as your Father. He is not like a human father, who is subject to different moods and is very limited in power. **You come to the heavenly Father who is always consistent, never changes, perfect in love and almighty in His power. His love for you will never falter and nothing is impossible for Him.**

You are not trying to catch Him in a good mood. He is merciful, which means that He never deals with us as we deserve. He is gracious, giving us the very opposite of what we deserve!

*And God is able to make all grace abound to you, so that in all things at all times, having all that you need, you will abound in every good work. (2 Corinthians 9: 8)*

You deserve nothing from God and can never earn His favour. You do not have to try to do this, for His nature is to be gracious towards you. He wants to supply whatever you need - always! This is His heart, the heart of your Father towards you.

**He wants you to expect to receive from Him, not on the basis of anything you have done, but because of His mercy, grace and love towards you!**

c) You will soon learn that it is the prayer of the heart that God answers - not some prayer that is a mere form of words. The words you speak are to be a true expression of what is in your heart. This is why it is necessary to have a time of prayer every day when you can pour out your heart to God.

He sees *"what is done in secret"* and He knows every thought, intention and desire of your heart! He wants to hear you express honestly what is in your heart; your longings, your fears and frustrations, your trust in Him to meet your need, to be with you in difficult situations, to provide abundantly for you in whatever way is appropriate.

**This is one of the most important and basic principles of prayer: to be totally honest with God.** There is no point in trying to impress Him or fool Him. You cannot convince Him that you believe when He can see the doubts that persist in your heart. Jesus makes this abundantly clear that God hates hypocrisy! He has no time for showy prayers that might impress others but make no impact on Him!

d) Jesus says that when the Father sees what you pray in secret, He *"will reward you"*. It is not a reward to say "No" to what you ask. He will only do that if you are asking for the wrong thing, or because He sees that you do not really expect Him to give to you in response to your prayer. God, your loving Father, will answer the true cry of your heart! So Jesus says:

> *"And when you pray, do not keep on babbling like pagans, for they think they will be heard because of their many words. Do not be like them, for your Father knows what you need before you ask him."* (Matthew 6: 7-8)

**The simple, honest cry of the heart is effective with God.** Streams of words that do not come from the heart are of no consequence. They might make a person feel good from a religious perspective, because he feels he has fulfilled an obligation or duty to pray; but such prayer is totally ineffective as far as God is concerned!

*"Your Father knows what you need before you ask him"*, Jesus says. If this is the case, what is the point of prayer? Why does God wait for us to ask before He gives what we need?

Think of the relationship between a human father and his child. There are certain basic needs the father provides consistently for the child, even though he or she does not ask. This is certainly true for us in relationship to God. He supplies in endless ways for us day by day, things that we take naturally for granted!

The human father, however, teaches the child to come and ask for whatever he lacks. He teaches the child not to demand, but to ask politely - reverently! However, the child also learns to ask with a natural kind of faith, expecting his father (or mother) to supply what is needed. He does not expect a rebuke if he is expressing a genuine need or if the 'treat' that he wants is within reason.

However the father is not a good father if he spoils the child granting his every demand. To do so would be damaging to the child. The loving parent gives the best he can in the best possible way out of love for the child.

Even so with our heavenly Father. He always wants to meet our genuine needs and often gives us 'treats' out of His love for us. But He will never spoil us or give what would have a negative effect on our lives.

Prayer is a relationship with your heavenly Father who loves you perfectly and is teaching you to trust in that love. **He knows your need, but He wants you to express your faith in His love by coming to Him humbly, yet confidently, expecting Him to meet the need.** Jesus says your Father *"will reward you",* when you do this.

# 3. THE LORD'S PRAYER

Jesus then gives us what is commonly known as 'The Lord's Prayer'. He is teaching His disciples *how* to pray, and never intended us to simply repeat these words like parrots, or in a religious way. He is showing His disciples what the content of their daily prayer needs to be.

It is good to take each phrase of the prayer and then to add your own words, praying from your heart, before proceeding to the next phrase. We will talk about how to do this later. Let us see now the *content* of the prayer, for this is the real point that Jesus is making to His disciples.

**OUR FATHER IN HEAVEN:**
God is your Father and Jesus tells you to address Him as such. Even though He wants you to have a close, intimate relationship with Him, He does not expect you to treat Him in a casual manner.

Nobody could have as close or intimate relationship with the Father as Jesus Himself during the time He spent on earth. Yet He did not speak to Him as 'Dad', but as 'Holy Father', and 'Righteous Father'.

Here Jesus tells us to address Him as 'heavenly Father'. In all these titles we are addressing the Holy One, who is awesome in majesty and glory, the One who is above all He has made, and yet the One who draws us close to Him in prayer.

**HE IS OUR HEAVENLY, HOLY, RIGHTEOUS FATHER!**

If you were invited to meet with a King, Queen or President, he or she might draw you into close conversation. A friendship could develop between you, but you would never forget the position and status of the one with whom you were building that relationship.

The Holy Spirit who lives within the believer urges us to address God as *"Abba, Father."* This is the intimate name a child would call his father, but in middle eastern culture it was always a term of deep respect as well as intimacy. We should never forget this. God does not want us to be afraid of Him as we would be of a stern disciplinarian, expecting to be corrected every time we approached Him. Yet He does not intend us to treat Him with casual disrespect. **He is our heavenly, holy, righteous Father!**

Being heavenly means that He is eternal; He can see equally what was, what is and what is to come. He knows the end from the beginning. He can see the future as clearly as He can see the past or the present.

This is difficult for us to understand because we live now within the limitations of time and space. Because God can see what will be, Jesus says His Spirit will tell us what is yet to come. So when God tells us what will be, or gives us a firm promise concerning the future, it will happen exactly as He said.

About 1000 years before the crucifixion Jesus, speaking from heaven, could explain to David the experience He was to have on the cross, even describing vividly some of the details. About 700 years before the event He described to Isaiah the significance as well as many of the details of the crucifixion.

So when you pray to the heavenly Father, He not only knows your need before you ask but also what He will do to meet the need. He is simply waiting for you to come into the secret place and express your need to Him!

**HALLOWED BE YOUR NAME:**
His name is holy and is to be revered. This underlines what has already been said, but makes it clear that worship and prayer belong together, true worship that is centred on the Lord Himself, seated in the glory of heaven, when His name is 'hallowed' continually. Day and night the creatures around His throne never stop saying:

> *"Holy, holy, holy is the Lord God Almighty, who was, and is, and is to come." (Revelation 4: 8)*

The elders lay their crowns before the throne and say:

> *"You are worthy, our Lord and God, to receive glory and honour and power, for you created all things, and by your will they were created and have their being." (Revelation 4: 11)*

And in heaven, the apostle John hears every creature in heaven and on earth singing:

*"To him who sits on the throne and to
the Lamb be praise and honour and glory and power,
for ever and ever!" (Revelation 5: 13)*

The Lamb is Jesus, who was sacrificed for us on the cross that we might know God as our Father and be made one with Him.

If this is how the heavenly host addresses the Lord, this is how we on earth should approach Him. The wonderful truth is that as great and awesome as He is, **we can approach His throne boldly and confidently because of the blood of Jesus that washes us from all our sins and makes us totally acceptable in His sight!**

The apostles, who had known Jesus personally when He was on earth, never addressed Him casually when they prayed; they were mindful of His greatness. They raised their voices together in prayer to God:

*"Sovereign Lord," they said,
"You made the heaven and the earth and the sea,
and everything in them ..." (Acts 4: 24)*

And yet they knew God as 'Father', and Jesus as their 'Lord', and 'Master', and 'Friend'.

It is good to begin your time of prayer by praising God, however briefly, for who He is and what He has done for us through Jesus.

## YOUR KINGDOM COME:

Jesus came with the gospel of the 'good news' of the Kingdom of God or the Kingdom of heaven. This Kingdom is the rule or reign of God within and among those who believe in Jesus. When you were born again, the Kingdom was planted within you as a seed that needs to develop, grow and bear fruit.

Jesus came to destroy the works of the devil, who had placed the whole world under his evil power. He came to rescue and save us from the dominion of darkness and to establish His reign, the rule of heaven here on earth. Because this is the heart of God's purpose, He tells us to pray for this to be fulfilled.

Now there is a very important principle implicit in what Jesus is telling us to do here. For He is saying **we are to pray for what God wants, for His purpose, before we come to any needs of our own.** Jesus promised:

> *But seek first his kingdom and his righteousness, and all these things will be given you as well. (Matthew 6: 33)*

You will not have to worry about anything, or about your needs, if you seek God's Kingdom first! This is the very heart of God's purpose, to see His heavenly Kingdom extended here on earth, for wherever He reigns His will shall be accomplished in the lives of those called to be His disciples.

## YOUR WILL BE DONE ON EARTH, AS IT IS IN HEAVEN:

This is an expansion of the previous phrase and shows us what it means to pray that God's Kingdom will come. If you are to pray this prayer from the heart (and there is no point in praying it otherwise) then you will want God's heavenly will for *your* life; you will want Him to rule and reign in the circumstances of *your* life.

In other words, it will become clear to others as well as yourself that you live devoted to God because you are intent on doing His will. Jesus said:

> *Not everyone who says to me, 'Lord, Lord,' will enter the kingdom of heaven, but only he who does the will of my Father who is in heaven. (Matthew 7: 21)*

There is no point in calling Jesus your Lord and praying for His will to be done, if you then live in deliberate disobedience to His will. This would undermine the effectiveness of your prayer, for that deliberate disobedience is an expression of what lies in your heart; and we know God looks on the heart when we pray.

> ... WE CANNOT DIVORCE OUR RELATIONSHIP WITH GOD IN PRAYER FROM THE REST OF OUR LIVES.

An earthly father is going to be reluctant in answering the request of his child if he or she is being deliberately disobedient, flaunting his authority. How much more so with God, our heavenly Father. This is why Jesus asked, *"Why do you call me, 'Lord, Lord,' and do not do what I say?" (Luke 6: 46)*

If Jesus is Lord of our lives He is the Boss! We are devoted to doing His will. This shows us that **we cannot divorce our relationship with God in prayer from the rest of our lives.** You do not only relate to a person when you are physically with that person. What you say about him or her at other times, the way you think about him or her, are all part of that relationship. So with our relationship with God.

This does not mean that we have to be in perfect obedience to God before He will answer our prayers! We can only live in obedience with His help gained *through* prayer! It is a matter of the heart. Notice that I used the phrase, *'deliberately'* disobey or *'deliberately'* sin. It is one thing to say 'No' to God in a deliberate act of defiance or rebellion, quite another to sin or fail through human weakness or frailty. In our weakness we need to depend on God.

If we are to pray with integrity we will seek to *do* His will. We will in effect be praying: *"Let your Kingdom come in my life. Let your will be done in my life as it is in heaven."*

Of course that is not the extent of our prayer, for we will also say, "Let your Kingdom be established in many who do not know you at present, who do not belong to your Kingdom. Lord, let your will be done in the lives of all who belong to you, who are already your children."

In this prayer, Jesus makes no specific mention of 'Church'; He speaks of His Kingdom, for **the calling of the Church is to extend the Kingdom here on earth; and to demonstrate the life of that heavenly Kingdom in the world** that still reveals so much influence of the evil one.

**GIVE US TODAY OUR DAILY BREAD:**
**Jesus intends us to pray every day!** This is clear from this statement. By 'bread' He means whatever we need each day, not only food. Whatever we need in order to live the life of God's Kingdom here on earth, to be fruitful and obedient to His will. He is the God of all grace who is able and wants to supply our every need.

He tells us to ask our heavenly Father for those needs to be met on a daily basis. *"Do not worry about your life, what you will eat or drink; or about your body, what you will wear." (Matthew 6: 25)* *"Therefore do not worry about tomorrow, for tomorrow will worry about itself. Each day has enough trouble of its own." (Matthew 6: 34)*

> HE WANTS YOU TO TRUST HIM ON A DAILY BASIS, BELIEVING HE WILL SUPPLY WHATEVER YOU NEED EACH DAY.

**Because God's concern is for you to live in a continual relationship of love with Him, He wants you to trust Him on a daily basis, believing He will supply whatever you need each day.** Tomorrow He will look after our needs tomorrow!

Worrying about the future never accomplishes anything and is a denial of our trust in the loving care of our heavenly Father. As we establish the practice of praying daily, we discover that God is faithful to His promises and undertakes for us on a daily basis.

If we do not turn to Him in prayer daily, it is no wonder that need can accumulate to such an extent that we then find it difficult to believe that God could change the situation.

**FORGIVE US OUR DEBTS:**
In Luke's version we read, *"Forgive us our sins". (Luke 11: 4)* Both are correct, for they point to our daily need of God's mercy.

Sin separates from God. Therefore we need His forgiveness, not only at the beginning of our Christian experience, but daily. Sin is anything in our lives that contravenes God's best purposes for us. It is unbelief and disobedience to His word and therefore His will!

When we come to the Lord in prayer, we do not want anything to stand between us, or to rob us of the effectiveness of our prayer. John says:

> *If we claim to be without sin, we deceive ourselves and the truth is not in us. If we confess our sins, he is faithful and just and will forgive us our sins and purify us from all unrighteousness. (1 John 1: 8-9)*

Unfortunately, none of us lives in sinless perfection; there are things that daily need to be forgiven. **Sin puts us in debt to God and others, and needs to be forgiven.** When we confess our sins they are forgiven!

To confess sins is to name them before God and seek His merciful pardon. It is not intended that we should be satisfied with a flippant or casual, "Forgive me all my sins, Lord." You need to face what those sins are specifically and not only seek His pardon, but also His grace to repent, to turn away from those particular things so you do not return to them or allow them to persist in your life. Without such repentance you will find yourself asking God to forgive the same offence again and again and again. And this becomes discouraging!

It is wonderful that God has accepted us in Jesus, that He will never condemn us, even for our repeated failures. His mercies are new every morning! When we confess our sins He will not beat or scold us; He will forgive us - not punish us. It is wonderful to know such mercy that spares you from having to live with the burden of guilt.

So it is definitely to your advantage that you ask for God's mercy and forgiveness whenever you pray. In fact you learn to ask for and receive immediate forgiveness by praying as soon as you become conscious of a particular sin. "Lord, please forgive me," is all that is needed in such a situation. You do not have to allow the burden of that sin to remain until your next scheduled time of prayer!

However, we are not immediately conscious of all sin that way. And so when we pray it is good to allow the Holy Spirit to show us any way in which we have grieved the Lord, so that we can be put right with Him, cleansed of all unrighteousness!

**AS WE ALSO HAVE FORGIVEN OUR DEBTORS:**
The version in Luke reads: *"For we also forgive everyone who sins against us" (Luke 11: 4).* We must never under-estimate the importance of what Jesus tells us to pray. **Because God is so merciful to us, He expects us to be merciful to others!** If we refuse, God will withhold His mercy from us. This would have disastrous consequences, for every answer to prayer is the work of His mercy and grace!

After giving the disciples 'The Lord's Prayer,' this is the part He immediately elaborated on:

> *For if you forgive men when they sin against you, your heavenly Father will also forgive you. But if you do not forgive men their sins, your Father will not forgive your sins. (Matthew 6: 14-15)*

Jesus taught such parables as 'The Unmerciful Servant,' to show the absolute necessity of forgiving those who sin against us, are indebted to us, or who have offended us in some way.

When Christians become offended because they have taken offence due to the way they have been treated, it is a very serious matter. People even leave churches due to offence instead of being obedient to God's Word and forgiving those who have caused the offence.

> TO FORGIVE IS NOT ALWAYS EASY, BUT IT IS ALWAYS NECESSARY.

**To forgive is not always easy, but it is *always* necessary.** When you forgive, the offence does not damage you in the way it does if you become bitter and resentful because you have refused to obey what Jesus says. Forgiveness is essentially a matter of the will, not of the emotions. You choose to forgive, even when you do not feel like forgiving the one who has grieved or offended you.

Sometimes the Lord allows offence in our lives to expose what is still in our hearts; by the way in which we react we see negative attitudes that we might never realise were present within us! Two Christians can respond to the same situation in completely different ways. One can be angry, bitter, resentful and offended; the other full of mercy and forgiveness because he has a merciful heart, so conscious is he of the Lord's mercy towards him.

The more you know God's mercy, the more likely you are to be merciful - and therefore more effective in prayer.

### AND LEAD US NOT INTO TEMPTATION:
The Greek can refer to any kind of trial or temptation. Some modern versions read: "Do not lead us into a time of trial."

The testing of our faith proves that it is genuine. We may need to go through testing times that the Lord might show us some negative streak that persists in our hearts. Sometimes it is a witness to others to see how, through God's grace, we are able to overcome in trying circumstances. At other times the Lord uses difficult situations to strengthen our trust in Him. All these consequences are positive; so clearly these are not the trials referred to here by Jesus.

Temptation is the enemy's way to try to lure us into sin. The Lord will never tempt us; the scriptures make this clear. Neither are we to put ourselves into a situation where we know we will find it difficult to resist temptation!

So it is right to ask the Lord not to lead us into any situation where temptation will arise, or any trial that will have a negative and destructive effect. We do not want to be open to the works of the enemy. Nor do we want to feel incapable of being able to resist or cope with the difficulties Satan would like to impose on us. It is right, therefore, that we should pray to be delivered from all the devices of the evil one. We want to prove faithful to the Lord!

**BUT DELIVER US FROM THE EVIL ONE:**
God has given us the shield of faith with which we are able to quench all the fiery darts the enemy fires at us. He has given us the sword of the Spirit, which is the word of God. Jesus overcame the devil's temptations in the wilderness by declaring scriptural truths; He overcame him by speaking the Word with authority.

At the same time, the Lord is a shield about us. How important, then, to pray that He will shield us from the thief who wants to steal, kill and destroy; a shield around us to protect us from sickness, premature death and every way in which the enemy would like to make us sin to undermine our witness and spiritual effectiveness!

**FOR YOURS IS THE KINGDOM AND THE POWER AND THE GLORY:**
This is known as the doxology and appears only in later manuscripts of the gospels. However, it is used commonly as part of 'the Lord's Prayer', and is certainly scriptural in content.

The Kingdom, remember, is God's primary purpose and the constant focus of the prayer. We pray to the Almighty One who has established His Kingdom on earth, a Kingdom and authority infinitely greater than anything the enemy can produce.

All glory belongs to our heavenly Father and to the Lamb, Jesus. As believers we are living in His overcoming power and to His glory. It would be utterly consistent with Jesus' teaching that we should end as we began, in praise of our God to whom belongs the Kingdom, the power to overcome, and the glory that belongs to Him for His victory, the victory He has already won on our behalf.

# 4

# ASK

Later in the Sermon on the Mount, Jesus returns to the theme of prayer:

*Ask and it will be given to you; seek and you will find, knock and the door will be opened to you. For everyone who asks receives; he who seeks finds; and to him who knocks, the door will be opened. (Matthew 7: 7-8)*

*"Ask and it will be given to you"*, seems so simple, and yet the experience of many (if not all at times) seems to undermine this promise. It could not be that Jesus was mistaken, nor that He was deliberately deceiving the early disciples. It seems even more incredible when He adds: *"For everyone who asks receives"*!

You may feel you want to protest by saying: "I have often asked God for things and I have not received. He has not done what I asked of Him!" Clearly, we need to seek clarification from other things that Jesus said concerning prayer. But first we need to understand that this is not a promise from Jesus for a 'quick fix' every time we are in need.

The Greek translated 'ask', literally means, 'Go on asking… Continue to ask…' It is a continuous tense expressing continuous action. Jesus taught that we should pray and never give up, no matter what the circumstances. So He does not mean that whatever we ask we shall immediately receive. And yet clearly He seems to suggest that the perseverance will certainly lead to the right conclusion.

Similarly, we are to go on seeking until we find. All who persist in seeking will find, Jesus promises. When we pray we do not always know what the answer should be to our dilemma. Persistence in prayer brings us through to the revelation we need, for the Holy Spirit can guide us as to *how* to pray and what we need to believe. True faith is often expressed in persistence, as with the widow in the parable:

> *Then Jesus told his disciples a parable to show them*
> *that they should always pray and not give up. He said:*
> *"In a certain town there was a judge who neither feared God nor*
> *cared about men. And there was a widow in that town who*
> *kept coming to him with the plea, 'Grant me justice*
> *against my adversary." (Luke 18: 1-3)*

Eventually the unjust judge said, *"I will see that she gets justice, so that she won't eventually wear me out with her coming!" (Luke 18: 5)* Her persistence was rewarded. Jesus concluded by saying:

> *Listen to what the unjust judge says. And will not*
> *God bring about justice for his chosen ones, who cry out*
> *to him day and night? Will he keep putting them off?*
> *I tell you, he will see that they get justice,*

> *and quickly. However, when the Son of Man comes, will he find faith on the earth? (Luke 18: 6-8)*

There are a number of significant things to learn here.

- When Jesus speaks of asking, He is speaking of being prepared to persist until we receive the answer. He is not referring to some superficial request, prayed with a kind of take it or leave it attitude, being prepared to accept any answer as being the right answer.

- God answers the prayer of the heart. This involves crying out to Him *"day and night"*. This is not some casual request reserved for the formal prayer time. The one who is praying will not be put off because he sees his need and knows only the Lord can answer that need. This is indeed true prayer.

- When there is such an expression of heart Jesus says the one praying will receive the answer quickly! Perseverance and determination produce quick results!

- Obviously Jesus regards such perseverance as the outworking or evidence of genuine faith, and He asks whether there will be evidence of such faith now or when He returns!

This raises an important issue: "What is the place of faith when we pray?"

# 5

# FAITH

Jesus makes a seemingly simple statement: *"If you believe, you will receive whatever you ask for in prayer." (Matthew 21: 22)* This does not need any interpretation; it is a clear promise from God. **When you pray, you will receive what you believe.**

Many people do not like to place such emphasis on faith, but it is unavoidable, for this is where Jesus Himself places the emphasis. We need only to look at other promises He gave concerning prayer to see this. He made a series of such promises at the Last Supper:

> *And I will do whatever you ask in my name, so that the Son may bring glory to the Father. You may ask me for anything in my name, and I will do it. (John 14: 13-14)*

- Jesus says that answered prayer will bring glory to the Father.

- He refers to every request you make of Jesus, using the words, *"whatever"* and *"anything"*.

- However, He uses the phrase, *"in my name"*. There must be an important key here, for He does not say that God promises to answer every prayer, but anything we ask *"in His name"*. This immediately begs the question as to what it means to pray in the name of Jesus.

Many would have used the name of Jesus when praying and still not seen the answer; so Jesus clearly means something different from using His name in the form of words used when praying. You may even have included the phrase, *"in the name of Jesus'"* and still not seen the answer. Jesus clearly does not mean that we reduce this to some formula tacked onto the end of our prayer, so that people know it is time to say, "Amen!" God, it seems, does not respond to using the name of Jesus as a formula. He throws further light on the matter for us:

*If you remain in me and my words remain in you,*
*ask whatever you wish, and it will be given you. This is to my*
*Father's glory, that you bear much fruit, showing yourselves*
*to be my disciples. (John 15: 7-8)*

- Again Jesus suggests that answered prayer gives glory to the Father. This must mean that He *wants* to answer our prayers!

- Jesus now speaks of receiving, *"whatever you wish,"* in prayer. This seems even more extraordinary, but even more removed from what many of us have experienced.

- The promise is as before, *"… it will be given to you."* Jesus does not say it might be given you, or could be, or may be, but *will* be given you!

- Receiving such answers will not only glorify the Father, but will be the evidence that we are disciples.

- However, there is this condition: *"If you remain in me and my words remain in you"*. What does Jesus mean by this? What does it mean to pray in the name of Jesus? What does it mean to abide in Him? What does it mean to say His words remain in you? Jesus also said:

> *You did not choose me, but I chose you and appointed you to go and bear fruit - fruit that will last. Then the Father will give you whatever you ask in my name. (John 15: 16)*

- Again Jesus is saying that answered prayer is connected to bearing fruit, which is what gives the Father glory in our lives.

- It seems that it does not matter whether you pray to Jesus or to the Father, so long as you ask in the name of Jesus!

- Again there is the promise that you will receive *whatever* you ask in His name! He later said:

> *I tell you the truth, my Father will give you whatever you ask in my name. Until now you have not asked for anything in my name. Ask and you will receive, and your joy will be complete. (John 16: 23-24)*

- When Jesus uses this phrase *"I tell you the truth"*, He knows His disciples will find what He is about to say difficult to accept or believe. Nevertheless it is definitely the truth!

- Answered prayer will bring us complete joy! We can all readily agree with that!

- Again He speaks of the Father giving us *whatever* we ask in His name. He is hammering home this truth again and again, clearly wanting the disciples to understand that when they were called and chosen, this is what God had in mind: that they would know Him as Father and believe that whatever they asked in Jesus' name they would receive.

So we are still left with this question as to what it means to ask in Jesus' name. The answer lies in the phrase, *"... if you abide in me and my words abide in you"*.

When you were born again, God took hold of your life and placed you 'in Christ Jesus'. Now everything that is His has become yours. You are a 'co-heir' with Christ and God has already blessed you in Him with every spiritual blessing in heavenly places. *(See Ephesians 1: 3)*

You are in the Vine of Jesus as a branch and cannot do anything apart from Him - including pray! You need His words to be abiding in you! The Greek translated as 'words' in this context is rhema, meaning that which God speaks *now,* His word for that particular time, the words the Holy Spirit brings as revelation to our hearts.

These 'spoken' words are as God's voice to us and will always be in total agreement with the logos, God's written unchangeable and perfect revelation of truth. Often the rhema is a logos that the Holy Spirit causes to 'come alive' for us at a particular moment, either when we are reading the scriptures, or a word that He brings to mind when we pray.

This is not taking a scripture and claiming it (as important as that is); it is God Himself taking the initiative. And this is the important point.

When you act in the name of someone else, you act on his behalf. You could not go into my bank and demand to withdraw some money from my account. You could *use* my name, saying that I sent you. Still the bank would not give you any money. However, if you took a cheque bearing my signature the bank clerk would know that I had initiated the transaction. You were truly asking for the money in my name.

All these scriptural promises of Jesus make sense. He is saying, **"I will do what I initiate, whatever I tell you to believe and ask for! When you hear what I say, believe me and ask accordingly, this brings glory to my Father, for I will only ever urge you to ask for that which will glorify Him and further His purpose in your life."**

Faith comes from hearing what Jesus says, and He promises that you will receive whatever you ask for in prayer *if you believe*. Now it is all adding together.

Whatever you ask according to His Word, the revelation of truth He gives, you will receive - whatever you wish. For His Word will never encourage you to feed your flesh or self life, in which nothing good dwells! He never encourages selfishness, even though He is ready to give abundantly to us.

There are a number of Christians who are adept at manipulating money from others, claiming to do this in the name of Jesus, whereas it is clear that their own fleshly desires are being satisfied! And they call this manipulation 'faith', promising people a great return for such giving. Such manipulation certainly does not glorify God, neither does it remotely correspond to what Jesus is promising at the Last Supper. He was not about to go to the cross so that some of His future servants could have a lavish, worldly lifestyle!

**Faith is faith in God and in what He says, responding to His initiative!** We ask 'in the name of Jesus' not as the repetition of a formula, but because we are responding to the initiative of the Holy Spirit. Paul says, therefore, that we are to pray at all times in the Spirit, certainly not in the flesh!

# 6

## HEARING FROM GOD

You need to hear from God to pray with the kind of faith of which Jesus speaks. This is not as difficult as many imagine. Every time you open your Bible and read you hear from God, and this needs to be an important part of your prayer time with the Lord every day: listening to what He says in the Bible.

Hearing God is not accomplished by legalistically reading a passage of scripture as a religious duty. Jesus tells us to take care how we hear. We need to read with listening hearts. It is wise to pray simply: "Holy Spirit speak to me now through the words of scripture."

As you read, He will give you understanding and will build and encourage your faith. Sometimes He will 'highlight' a particular phrase, verse or passage that is a prophetic word from God to you at that time. When this occurs it seems this particular truth jumps out of the page and hits you in the heart. It is as if that verse has just been put into your Bible, or as if you had never noticed it before. Suddenly it takes on new meaning. It is important to respond to such revelation in prayer, for the Holy Spirit only works like this for a reason. He has highlighted that verse at that time for some specific reason! God is speaking to you and that is an essential, perhaps the most important, aspect of prayer.

I would guess that only about ten percent of my daily prayer time is spent talking to the Lord. Ninety percent of the time I am listening to what He is saying to me through His written Word and by His Spirit.

If you spend some time first reading the scriptures and then write down what you believe God is saying to you by His Spirit, you will find it much easier to maintain concentration. I find it helpful to highlight the biblical text as I read. Again this helps concentration. I keep a daily journal of what I believe that God then says to me.

Of course the journal does not have the same level of inspiration as scripture and should not be treated as such, for Paul says our prophecy is imperfect. And this is a form of prophecy, which is essentially God speaking to His people. In scripture we hear God perfectly, in our personal revelation imperfectly. However you will find keeping a journal of immense value. At least once a week go back over what you believe the Lord has said, and you will find that you have heard some things clearly from the Spirit, clear enough to write them down, things that He repeats again and again. You then realise that you have listened but not acted on these words. **The Holy Spirit is lovingly and patiently holding them before you again and again until you take these words to heart and act on them obediently.**

When we listen to the Lord in this way, He gives us further understanding of His Word, the words of scripture. He can also warn us of impending danger or caution that is needed. These inner promptings of the Spirit, often known as the witness of the Holy Spirit, are a precious part of His ministry to us and are not to be ignored. The Lord never warns us without just cause.

This is one of His ways of keeping us out of temptation and the snares the devil lays for us. So be wise and take heed of what He says. He will never inspire fear, for He has not given us a Spirit of fear, but of power, of love and of a sound mind. When He warns you and you heed what He says, you go forward confidently, trusting Him, knowing that He will keep your feet from evil!

**Prayer is the language of relationship with God.** It always seems to me that it is more important for me to listen to Him than to spend the time expecting Him to listen to me. Of course I need to ask and believe. But I can ask with much greater confidence and faith having spent much time listening to Him, for faith comes from hearing God speaking through His Word and by His Spirit!

You need to understand that if you have received the Holy Spirit, it is not difficult for you to 'hear' God speaking to you! Do not expect to hear an audible voice. He is Spirit, and He will speak to your spirit, your inner man, the deep innermost part of your being. Test everything you 'hear' by God's Word, for the Holy Spirit will never speak anything that either contradicts scripture or that is not in complete harmony with God's Word. Jesus said:

> *But when he, the Spirit of truth, comes, he will guide you into all truth. He will not speak on his own; he will speak only what he hears, and he will tell you what is yet to come. He will bring glory to me by taking from what is mine and making it known to you. (John 16: 13-14)*

**Even when you are not listening to heaven, the Holy Spirit within you is!** He wants to tell you what the Father and Jesus are saying, more than you desire to hear His voice. If God has such a desire to speak to you, then it will not be difficult to hear what He is saying. You simply need to give yourself time to listen and learn to recognise the voice of the Spirit from all the other thoughts that can afflict your mind.

**Not all the thoughts you have when you pray will come from God. This is why it is essential to test everything by God's Word of truth.** If the devil spoke to Jesus and the early Christians, he will find ways of trying to distract you from God's purposes. However, you do not need to live in fear of the enemy, for God has given you authority over all the power of the evil one.

# 7. AUTHORITY TO HAVE VICTORY

God is your Father; Jesus is your Lord and Friend; the devil is your enemy. **All that God does for you and in you is good, right and wholesome.** Everything your enemy desires for you is bad, wrong and destructive. He is the very opposite of Jesus and his purposes always oppose God's best plans for your life.

Because you are on the Lord's side you pray to the One who cares for you and wants the very best for you. **On the cross Jesus overcame all the negatives that are the work of the enemy!**

*Surely he took up our infirmities and carried our sorrows. (Isaiah 53: 4)*

*He was pierced for our transgressions, he was crushed for our iniquities; the punishment that brought us peace was upon him, and by his wounds we are healed. (Isaiah 53: 5)*

*The LORD has laid on him the iniquity of us all. (Isaiah 53: 6)*

*He was oppressed and afflicted. (Isaiah 53: 7)*

> *Yet it was the LORD's will to crush him and
> cause him to suffer. (Isaiah 53: 10)*

> *After the suffering of his soul, he will see the light of life
> and be satisfied. (Isaiah 53: 11)*

In these extracts from just one passage of scripture about the cross, we can see how Jesus dealt with all the negative things that can afflict us, everything that the enemy wants to encourage in your life. What a list of things Jesus has done!

- He overcame all your infirmities.

- He carried all your grief and sorrow.

- He overcame your transgressions, all the ways in which you have disobeyed God and sinned against Him.

- He was crushed to free you from everything that causes you to feel crushed, including that crushing weight of guilt.

- He suffered the punishment that you deserve so that you will not be punished by God, but can be the recipient of His love, mercy and grace.

- He made it possible for you to have peace, instead of the conflict, disorder and confusion the enemy brings by trying to make God's children feel condemned.

- He took *all* your sin on Himself, so that you can be clean in God's sight and can have confidence before Him when you pray.

- He accomplished your healing when He was wounded for your sake.

- He was oppressed to free you from whatever oppression the devil might try to inflict on you.

- He was afflicted so you can be healed and delivered.

- He hung on that cross so that no matter what causes you to feel crushed could be dealt with.

- He suffered in His soul to liberate you from whatever negatives can afflict your soul life.

- He had *"no beauty or majesty to attract us to him, nothing in his appearance that we should desire him"*. *(Isaiah 53: 2)* He even identified with all those who feel unattractive, undesirable and unwanted, to make them acceptable to God, chosen by Him to be His beloved children and co-heirs with Christ.

> ... IT IS ALWAYS IMPORTANT TO PRAY IN LINE WITH GOD'S WORD.

Why have we looked at those scriptures? Because **it is always important to pray in line with God's Word.** We need to know, therefore, what He has done for us through Jesus.

Our prayer will be ineffective if we are asking Him to do what He has already done. In effect that would be to pray with unbelief, not faith, or in ignorance of the Word that inspires faith. And we have seen that Jesus promised that every prayer of faith would be answered. As we can only pray with faith in line with God's Word, it is essential to be men and women of the Word, if we are going to be serious about prayer.

We can benefit greatly from books that bring us to a greater understanding of God's Word and to a living faith. Not all Christian books do this. Those written by men and women of faith will inspire faith in others. If you need healing, for example, you do not want a theoretical view of the subject, but to read what has been written by one whom God has used significantly in the healing of others! Such people will keep your focus on Jesus and what He has done on the cross. They will help you come to a greater appreciation of the spirit, life and power that are in God's Word.

These scriptures show us that Jesus has already overcome all these negatives on the cross. He has given us immense authority as believers, authority that is to be expressed in prayer. Jesus said:

*I saw Satan fall like lightning from heaven. (Luke 10: 18)*

**Because your citizenship is now in heaven, and you belong to the Kingdom of God, you have authority over the works of the one who has been thrown out of heaven for his pride and rebellion against the authority of God.** So Jesus continues:

*I have given you authority ... to overcome all the power of the enemy; nothing will harm you. (Luke 10: 19)*

The reason you can overcome is that Jesus, in whom you live and who lives in you by His Spirit, has already overcome all the works of the enemy on the cross. **You are not trying to overcome the** devil in your own strength, but applying the victory Jesus has already accomplished over the devil and all his works.

Faith takes hold of that victory in prayer and applies it. This does not happen through the repetition of a formula: "I bind you, Satan." If that formula were effective, Satan would have been rendered powerless long ago, so many Christians use it!

**No, the scriptures are clear, it is the exercise of our faith that gives us the authority to overcome, faith in the victory Jesus has already won!** So He says:

> *"I tell you the truth, whatever you bind on earth*
> *will be bound in heaven, and whatever you loose on earth*
> *will be loosed in heaven." (Matthew 18: 18)*

It is not easy to translate the Greek simply. Jesus is saying that we have the authority to bind (to hinder or prevent) on earth what is already bound (hindered or prevented) in heaven. When we exercise the authority to bind on earth, all heaven is behind us because those things are already bound in heaven, the Kingdom to which we belong.

In like manner we have the authority to loose (to release) on earth whatever is released in heaven. Again, when we exercise that authority all heaven is behind us and acts on our behalf.

Now we are learning something different about prayer: it is not only a matter of speaking to God, but of speaking to 'mountains', to problems or needs. It is exercising authority over the powers of darkness that seek to hinder us and others.

There is no point in thinking that you do not want to exercise such authority. Unless you do, the enemy will be able to afflict you in one way after another. Even as you read this you may realise that this has already been the case in the past. You have been defeated in some ways because you have not exercised authority over the works of the enemy.

**Miraculous things will happen when you listen to the voice of God and speak to the situation in His name.** He maintains the initiative, showing you what to believe and do - through His Word and by His Spirit. And this is still prayer!

One of the most remarkable miracles in the Bible occurred when Joshua commanded the sun to stand still, remarkable for God would have had to suspend the laws of the universe for a period for this to happen, otherwise there would literally have been universal chaos. The scripture records:

> *On the day the LORD gave the Amorites over to Israel, Joshua said to the LORD in the presence of Israel: "O sun, stand still over Gibeon, O moon, over the valley of Aijalon." So the sun stood still, and the moon stopped, till the nation avenged itself on its enemies.*
> *(Joshua 10: 12-13)*

> MIRACULOUS THINGS WILL HAPPEN WHEN YOU LISTEN TO THE VOICE OF GOD AND SPEAK TO THE SITUATION IN HIS NAME.

The text says that Joshua spoke to the Lord; yet he addressed the sun and moon instead! Clearly Joshua was acting in obedience to what God was leading him to do, for God would not suspend the laws of the universe unless it was

His will to do so. He would not do such a thing on the whim of a man, not even Joshua!

No wonder, *"There has never been a day like it before or since, a day when the LORD listened to a man". (verse 14).* God listened to Joshua expressing faith as he spoke to the sun and the moon. God will inspire whatever faith is necessary for you to be bold in prayer. Joshua spoke to the 'mountain', and Jesus tells us to do likewise.

The enemy causes all kinds of hindrances in the lives of God's people, things that seem like mountains blocking the way ahead. Many speak *about* the mountains rather than *to* them. They even pray to the Lord *about* them; instead of obeying His Word to speak to the mountains and command them to move. Jesus makes it clear that when we speak to mountains of need, we must believe in our hearts that they will be moved.

> *I tell you the truth, if anyone says to this mountain, "Go, throw yourself into the sea," and does not doubt in his heart but believes that what he says will happen, it will be done for him. (Mark 11: 23)*

- Jesus is speaking about 'anyone' who believes, any one of His children.

- The 'mountain' is a work of the enemy, for God would not create mountains and then tell us to speak to them to have them moved!

- There is no point in speaking to a 'mountain' if you expect nothing to happen as a result, or you have doubts about whether the problem will be resolved.

- Jesus says that the one praying must believe *"... that what he says will happen"*. Can you see that if we are praying in the Spirit, truly in the name of Jesus, following His leading, then we will *know* that the mountain will be moved because He is taking the initiative?

It is for this reason that Paul says that God always leads us in His triumphal procession in Christ Jesus. **He will never lead us in fear, failure and defeat. He is the answer in every situation.** Following His leading, praying, speaking and acting in His name, establishes His victory in the situation.

- Jesus does not say you have to move the mountain, only speak to it in faith. He promises that "it will be done for" you! He continues:

*Therefore I tell you, whatever you ask for in prayer, believe that you have received it, and it will be yours. (Mark 11: 24)*

Again that emphasis on faith! In fact this passage is often called 'The Prayer of Faith.'

Jesus gives us a clear sequence.

1) **He says,** *"Have faith in God"*, the Lord, the Almighty One for whom nothing is impossible; the Father who loves you, cares for you and wants to meet your need.

2) **He tells us to speak to the mountain, believing that it will be moved.** Having seen the situation from God's perspective we see that now it is not impossible or immeasurable!

3) **We are to believe that we have received the unseen,** in which case we will give thanks to God for the victory we have through Jesus.

4) **Jesus then emphasised the need to forgive others if our prayer is to be effective.** Sometimes you will need to forgive those whom the enemy has used to cause the mountain in the first place! This is not always easy, but it is necessary:

> *And when you stand praying, if you hold anything against anyone, forgive him, so that your Father in heaven may forgive you your sins. (Mark 11: 25)*

It is written in this context of addressing mountains that Jesus makes this comprehensive statement: *"If you believe, you will receive whatever you ask for in prayer"* (Matthew 21: 22). To Jesus this is a necessary and indispensable part of prayer. How sad, therefore, that many Christians have never been taught this or how to do it. It is even more powerful when we pray with such faith and authority in agreement with others, for Jesus also said:

> *Again, I tell you that if two of you agree about anything you ask for, it will be done for you by my Father in heaven. (Matthew 18: 19)*

**Obviously Jesus is speaking about agreeing in faith, in expectation, in the exercise of the authority He has given us as believers.**

Sadly many believe that to pray about the problem is sufficient. This is hardly in accord with what Jesus teaches. Many spend a few minutes thinking about their problems and say "Amen" at the end. This to them is prayer. I do not say this in judgment, but out of concern, for it shows that they have never been given revelation of the importance of faith, or of how to exercise authority in prayer!

There is certainly no power in thinking or talking *about* your problems. In fact, the more you do this, the greater the problems seem to become! The perseverance in prayer that Jesus speaks of is to be a perseverance in faith. Those who bear a hundred fold fruit are *"those with a noble and good heart, who hear the word, retain it, and by persevering produce a crop" (Luke 8:15).*

# 8

## NO CONDEMNATION

It is important to realise that there is no condemnation for what we might regard as past failures in prayer. When anyone opens up the Word in faith, as I have done above, he or she is often accused of condemning those who have prayed with great sincerity, but with little success, especially in the realm of healing.

Of course I am condemning no one; that is solely the work of the devil! Unless we open up the Word in faith, we will never learn to pray with faith and be effective. **Remember, God is glorified by the prayers that produce answers - and this is what we all want, both to glorify the Father and to see our prayers being effective.**

> REMEMBER, GOD IS GLORIFIED BY THE PRAYERS THAT PRODUCE ANSWERS

A person can only pray according to the revelation he or she had at any specific time. God does not condemn us for a lack of revelation; but does want to increase continually the revelation of the truth in our hearts and lives. There is no point in looking back to the past with regret. Any of our past failures need to inspire us to seek to be more effective in prayer in the future.

The problem for some is that they do not pray consistently but wait until they are confronted by a major need, and then wonder why they lack the faith and authority to pray with power. **If we live in a faith relationship with Jesus, many problems would not be able to take root in our lives.** For at the first signs of trouble, we would recognise the work of the enemy and refuse to accept the things he wants to put upon us. Even many sicknesses begin with a negative thought which, if received, is followed by another negative and another until there is an expectation of sickness. That is tantamount to saying the person has had faith to become sick, because he or she has listened to the negative seeds sown by the enemy.

Of course not all sickness comes upon people in this way, but some does. It is difficult to suddenly swivel from an expectation of sickness to an expectation that God will certainly heal. If a person has a negative mind-set about anything it is very difficult to suddenly change to a positive mind-set. It is necessary to ask the Lord to forgive the negative unbelief and to sow good, positive seeds of revelation of the truth of His Word.

> IF WE LIVE IN A FAITH RELATIONSHIP WITH JESUS, MANY PROBLEMS WOULD NOT BE ABLE TO TAKE ROOT IN OUR LIVES.

The Lord does not condemn, nor should any believer judge another. It is a total lack of love to say to someone: "You did not receive your healing because you did not believe". Even if this is true, we are called upon to encourage faith in one another, the strong helping the weak.

However, there is no point in teaching people methods of prayer unless it is clearly understood that, regardless of the method, faith in God has to be at the heart of all our praying. **Our focus has to be on Him, not ourselves, or the problem, or the need.** Even when we speak to the mountain our expectation is to be that God will move it!

> OUR FOCUS HAS TO BE ON HIM, NOT OURSELVES, OR THE PROBLEM, OR THE NEED.

So prayer is not to be a nice, spiritual exercise, nor a religious duty. It is to be the effective way in which we strengthen our relationship of faith in God through Jesus Christ, faith in His love, faith working through love. That, Paul says, is the only thing that counts.

If you have any regrets about past events, bring them before the Lord immediately. Thank Him for His love and mercy, that He has forgiven you for any failure or unbelief on your part, that in His love for you He has carried you through all these past dilemmas, that He is with you now, nothing can separate you from His love for you in Christ Jesus, and that He is going to lead you on in His purposes, enabling you to pray with greater faith and boldness in the future.

**Jesus does not condemn you. In His love He died for you to save you from condemnation.**

# 9
## THE NEED OF DISCIPLINE

In order to have an effective prayer life, to build your relationship with Jesus in prayer, you need to learn to be disciplined in prayer.

Your flesh, your natural self-life, does not want to pray and the enemy will do anything he can to prevent you from praying, for he knows that it is only through prayer that he will be overcome in your life. It is for these reasons, unless you are disciplined, prayer will drop down your list of priorities. You will keep putting off your time devoted to the Lord, putting other things first. Before you know where you are you have become so busy and preoccupied that you think you have no time to pray.

It is never true to say that you have no time to pray. God has given you twenty-four hours in every day, and if you cannot give Him a period of at least 20-30 minutes in that time then you have your priorities totally wrong! The one who does not pray has no revelation of the importance of prayer, or the power of God that would be released in and through his or her life if only there were a disciplined prayer life.

Like many other things in life, the more practice we have the more able we become. It would be pointless picking up a musical instrument for the first time and putting it aside in disgust because you were unable to play it well after only a few days. If you are determined to master the instrument, you will keep playing to become more accomplished.

Prayer is much like this. Why be disappointed if you have not mastered it in a few days? How determined are you to improve the quality of your relationship with Jesus? How serious are you about learning *how* to pray with faith so that you can be a blessing to others as well as yourself - to your family, friends, work-associates and others who are in any need? Do you not realise that it is a great expression of love to be able to pray for people, especially those who are close to you?

The best time to pray is first thing in the morning, before you become pre-occupied with other things! Then, you will be fresh and able to concentrate instead of your mind drifting onto other issues. This is a general rule, but it cannot be universally applied. Mothers with young children often find it better to pray during the baby's morning sleep period. Some people do not truly wake up until they have been up for some time! Night owls find concentration easier late at night.

You need to do what is right for you. However, unless you have a regular time in prayer, and are disciplined in keeping to that, you will find that you 'miss' your prayer time again and again.

Look at it like this. You have a daily appointment with Jesus and no one could be more important than Him. **So don't stand Him up! He is waiting for you at the appointed time!**

# 10

# METHODS

There are many ways of putting these basic principles of prayer into action. It is important to find the ways that suit you best, and not be stuck religiously or legalistically with one method.

For example over the years I have taught our Bible College students and others different methods that have transformed their prayer lives. They never appreciated that it was possible to meet with God and receive from Him in such ways, because no one had taught them these things previously.

When trying a different method of prayer, give yourself time to adjust to it. Remember the musical instrument; you will not be an expert the first time you play it! No matter what the method, we must always pray with the heart and in faith. These are two essentials in every kind of prayer.

**RECEIVING FROM GOD**
The Lord not only wants to speak to you; He wants you to receive from Him. This is not difficult, if you know *how* to receive. God wants to give to you even more than you desire to receive from Him! Jesus tells us that there is spirit and life in God's Word itself.

**You can therefore take His words and receive the spirit and life that is in them. He said:**

> *When you enter a house, first say, 'Peace be to this house.'*
> *If a man of peace is there, your peace will rest on him; if not,*
> *it will return to you. (Luke 10: 5-6)*

"Peace be to this house" is more than a greeting. It is a blessing, words that actually convey God's peace. That peace has to go somewhere once it is spoken. If it is not received by the man in the house it will come upon you!

When Jesus appeared to the disciples in His risen body, they were shut away in fear. He greeted them with the words: *"Peace be with you!"* He wanted His peace to come upon them. This was not simply a greeting, but an impartation of peace. Earlier Jesus had promised the disciples:

> *Peace I leave with you; my peace I give you. I do not give*
> *to you as the world gives. Do not let your hearts be troubled*
> *and do not be afraid. (John 14: 21)*

The blessing of God's peace is in these words; they are eternal and contain the life of His Spirit. **You can receive that peace any time you choose to do so, whether in your prayer time or even if you are in the middle of a stressful situation.** This peace is supernatural and *"passes all understanding"*, Paul says.

Sit down quietly and simply repeat to yourself, or aloud if you are alone, the words, "Peace I leave with you; my peace I give you." Repeat these words slowly a number of times, as if Jesus Himself were speaking them to you - and God's peace will descend on you. You will be surprised how simple it is to receive this peace!

I use this as an example, but God's Spirit and life is in *all* scripture. **You can take any other appropriate verse and receive the life that God wants to impart to you through that truth.** This is not an exercise of your mind, but of your spirit. Do not try to reason what the scripture means; simply receive the life it contains! Do not try to empty your mind; that is an activity associated with the occult. Simply focus your attention on Jesus and know He is speaking His words to you.

In my book, 'Listen and Live' I describe fully this powerful way of receiving from God and show how you can convey His life and power to others by using the scriptures in this way. It is particularly appropriate to use scriptures associated with the names of God and of Jesus. For example:

*I am the LORD who heals you (Exodus 15: 26)*
*I am the LORD who provides (Genesis 22: 14)*
*I am the LORD your shepherd; you shall not want (Psalm 23: 1)*
*I am the LORD your peace (Judges 6: 24)*
*I am the LORD who is present; I will never leave you nor forsake you. (Deuteronomy 31: 6/ Joshua 1: 5)*
*As the Father has loved me, so have I loved you (John 15: 9)*

You can see from these few examples that this kind of prayer -

- Helps you focus on the Lord and His provision.

- Repeating such Scriptural truth will encourage and strengthen your faith.

- You can receive different aspects of God's love and life.

- You can take two scriptures and put them together.

- It helps you to receive by personalising the scriptural verse.

For example, David says, *"The Lord is my shepherd; I shall not want."* You can use that as an affirmation of faith or you can say, "I am the Lord your shepherd; you shall not want." I find it helpful to know that the Lord is speaking His Word to me personally in this way.

I carry around a number of these scriptures written on a piece of paper inserted in my Bible. At any moment I can sit down and receive from the Lord in this way. As part of my time daily with the Lord I spend time receiving from Him through a number of scriptures that are appropriate for me personally. And I pray for others in this way, conveying to them in the Spirit, the life and power of His Word. I simply add the name of the person to the appropriate scripture and spend a few moments believing that as I speak these words over that person's life, so God works in them. For example I might pray, "I am the Lord who heals you, George," repeating this a number of times, believing that God's healing power embraces him as I pray.

You see, faith has to operate no matter what method of prayer you use. You are not simply to repeat words, but believe that you are conveying life and healing in the name of Jesus. This is one way of healing the sick, rather than simply praying for the sick!

## PRAYING OVER SCRIPTURES

Another profitable way to use scripture in prayer is to take a short passage and pray over each phrase, expanding this in prayer as you do so. You can apply the verses you use to yourself, to others, to the Church or the nation even.

For example, you could use Isaiah 61: 1-3 phrase by phrase. You could begin in this way: **"The Spirit of the Sovereign Lord is on me.** I thank you, Lord, for the gift of your Spirit, I believe your Spirit is upon me and upon your Church. I pray that your body will be revived by the power of your Spirit and that this nation will experience a significant move of your Spirit that will bring many into your Kingdom. **Because the Lord has anointed me.** I thank you, Lord Jesus, that you have anointed me personally, that your hand is on me and your power at work within me to enable me to fulfil your purpose for my life. I pray for continual anointing on the church to which I belong that we will be increasingly effective in reaching the world with your gospel ..." and so on for the rest of this short passage.

This is another powerful way of prayer because it keeps your prayer in total agreement with God's Word. And there is more power in His Word than in your words! Also this is a wonderful way of praying prophetic scriptures into being.

This method can be used corporately, encouraging each person to pray over the same passage at the same time. Sometimes hundreds of people are doing this at Kingdom Faith, before the leader of the meeting sums up the prayer corporately.

## PRAYING IN THE SPIRIT

We have seen that the Holy Spirit needs to operate in our prayer at all times. As He points us to God's Word, you will find He works powerfully through both the methods of prayer outlined above. **We are told to** *"... pray at all times in the Spirit"*. Paul explains:

> *The Spirit helps us in our weakness. We do not know what we ought to pray for, but the Spirit himself intercedes for us with groans that words cannot express. (Romans 8: 26)*

There are many occasions when we do not know how to pray, or what is right to ask God to do. The gift of speaking in tongues is very useful at such times. Through this gift the Holy Spirit prays in and through you, beyond your understanding. He always knows the right way to pray and what to believe, no matter what the situation. Paul says, *"I will pray with my spirit, but I will also pray with my mind"* (1 Corinthians 14: 15).

There have been numerous times when I have been utterly perplexed. As I have begun to pray in the language the Spirit has given me, I begin to understand the way He is leading me to pray and believe. I go from tongues to English, back to tongues, then to English and so on. I am praying with my spirit and with my mind also.

However there are times when the Holy Spirit will move us to pray totally beyond our understanding, and it is then that you can find yourself groaning in the Spirit. It is as if He has placed a burden of prayer on you, to pray about a particular situation, and you sense that you have to continue to pray until He gives you relief and the groaning is replaced by a sense of peace. Even though you may not understand what has taken place, you simply know that you have fulfilled an important task in prayer that the Holy Spirit gave you.

We must certainly not limit our prayer to our very limited understanding. When we pray we are touching the realm of the Spirit, of the supernatural, where often things are beyond our understanding!

If you have been baptised in the Holy Spirit the gift of speaking in tongues is waiting to be expressed through you. **Believe you have received the gift and you will be able to use it!**

You will also be able to benefit from other gifts of the Spirit as you pray. Through words of knowledge God can show you what the real problem is in a situation and what He is prepared to do in it if you believe. Through words of wisdom He can show you *how* to pray about a certain matter. Through words of prophecy, He tells you what He is speaking into a particular situation. This is particularly important. For if we are to pray with faith, and faith comes from hearing the Lord's spoken word to our hearts, it is important to know what He is saying about the subject of our prayer. Even when speaking, we need to be listening, so that we can allow the Holy Spirit to direct our prayer.

## MEDITATION

When we meditate we use the mind, but under the inspiration of the Holy Spirit. There has to be a focus of our meditation, a verse or passage of scripture so that our thinking is centred on the truth!

It is not a matter of trying to work out the meaning of a particular scripture with our limited understanding, but of asking the Holy

Spirit to speak to us through those words, *giving us revelation of the truth*. In this way you will understand far more than trying to work out the meaning for yourself.

However, it is important to ask the Holy Spirit to direct you to the scriptures on which you are to meditate, otherwise you will sometimes be very frustrated. God has His timetable in every one of our lives, and there is no point in asking Him to give you understanding of something that has no bearing on His purpose for your life at that particular time. Certainly you must avoid any temptation to try to work out when Jesus will return. Only the Father knows that, and many Christians have wasted hours of valuable time trying to work out with their minds what the Spirit has no intention of revealing!

**DRAW NEAR TO THE THRONE**
God Himself must always be the focus of our prayer, no matter what method we adopt. He wants to reveal Himself to us and draw us close to Him, to His throne:

> *Let us then approach the throne of grace with confidence, so that we may receive mercy and find grace to help us in our time of need. (Hebrews 4: 16)*

This is the place of effective prayer: before God's throne. It is worth spending time drawing near to Him before we start asking for ourselves or interceding for others. There are a number of ways we can draw near to the throne:

- We can come through the 'gates of thanksgiving', and into the 'courts of praise'. There is continual praise surrounding God's throne. You can begin your time of prayer by thanking God for the blessings of His mercy and grace, before entering into a time of praise. Only then you can make requests of Him!

- Through repentance: Others like to begin by cleansing their hearts before the Lord. "Who may ascend the hill of the LORD? Who may stand in his holy place? He who has clean hands and a pure heart." (Psalm 24: 3-4) The throne is where the Holy One reigns.

- You can use the method of receiving from God through His Word, for this brings you into the awareness of His Presence with you.

- Or you can simply believe that because of your position in Christ you stand in the grace of God before the throne and you know that He will hear whatever you say to Him.

Personally, I use all these ways of approaching the throne of God, according to which is the most appropriate at any given time. They all 'work', bringing you to that place where you can approach the throne 'with confidence'. There you will find mercy, which means that you will receive God's forgiveness for whatever has grieved Him, and grace according to your need. **He will give to you in exactly the right way, and will undertake for you, no matter what the situation.**

It is good to know that you have placed yourself and your needs in the Lord's hand. This is important, that before His throne you worship Him and yield yourself afresh to Him.

When you place yourself at arm's length from the Lord's loving embrace, you limit what He wants to do in you. There are no safer hands to be in, and this act of surrendering yourself to Him inspires the confidence and security of having your life in His keeping!

## INTERCESSION

Before God's throne, you will be concerned, not only to pray for yourself, but also for other people and situations. This kind of prayer is called 'intercession' - standing before God on behalf of others, asking of Him for their benefit.

> SOMETIMES YOU WILL NEED TO EXERCISE SPIRITUAL AUTHORITY OVER THOSE FOR WHOM YOU PRAY.

Obviously we pray regularly like this for those we love, for our local church and leaders, those involved with us in our work life and so on. There are always sick people to pray for and others in various kinds of need.

Again, we can employ different methods of prayer in intercession, using the principles about which we have already spoken. Again we must pray from the heart, not simply out of a sense of duty, for it is the heart that God looks upon and answers. And we pray with faith, believing that we impart blessing to those for whom we pray in the name of Jesus.

**Sometimes you will need to exercise spiritual authority over those for whom you pray.** For example, when praying for lost souls who do not know Jesus personally, it is good to take authority over the god of this age that has blinded the minds of unbelievers and pray that they will be able to receive the light of revelation from God's Spirit and Word.

Sometimes when praying for the sick, you sense it is necessary to take authority over spirits of infirmity that have afflicted a particular person. Without using such authority when appropriate, prayers for healing will not be effective. Jesus said we are to speak to the mountains before asking and believing for God to be active in the situation.

The believer with the problem has the responsibility to speak to his or her own mountains. However, you can stand with a believer in doing this, either when you pray for him or with him. Remember, using the authority God gives you is one aspect of faith!

Do not try to intercede for too many people at once, unless you are called to a ministry of intercession. It is better to pray meaningfully for a few people each day than pray superficially for a long list of people! It is always important to end your prayer, either for yourself or others, with thanksgiving, as Jesus did:

> *"Father, I thank you that you have heard me.*
> *I knew that you always hear me."*
> *(John 11: 41-42)*

These are words I use frequently, for if I pray with faith I know the Lord has heard me and that He has, therefore, answered me. John writes:

> *This is the confidence we have in approaching God:*
> *that if we ask anything according to his will, he hears us.*
> *And if we know that he hears us - whatever we ask -*
> *we know that we have what we asked of him.*
> *(1 John 5: 14-15)*

This is the confidence the Holy Spirit gives us. You know that you know that you know that the Lord has heard and that He undertakes to deal with the matter, even if there is no immediate visible change in the circumstances. You can be at peace because you know He has undertaken!

## 11

## CORPORATE PRAYER

Much of what has been said in this short book has been directed at the personal prayer of the believer. Of course it is the responsibility of every congregation to be a people of prayer. It is sad that often the church prayer meeting is attended by only a few. However, this is understandable if such meetings are boring, more or less a repetition of the same people saying the same prayers on each occasion. Often they pray in such a way that you wonder whether people are speaking to the Lord or to others present! The whole thing has descended to the level of a religious exercise instead of being an exciting and vibrant time of meeting with God.

The way in which corporate prayer meetings are led is of great importance. And often it is necessary and helpful to give some brief teaching on *how* to pray, especially if inexperienced believers are present! It should not be presumed that everyone knows how to pray.

Hopefully, the pastors will be people of prayer. If not, those with an anointing on their prayer life should lead. It is better to be led by anointing than by someone who has a position, but no anointing for leading prayer! If pastors are not people of prayer they should become so, for they cannot fulfil their ministries properly unless they are praying men or women!

The same principles apply to corporate prayer: it must come from the heart and be an expression of faith. It is difficult to engage your heart with God if you are only listening to others pray. It is much more effective if the leader sets the faith objective, and then everyone is given liberty to pray out loud in their own words from their hearts and at the same time. This is very powerful. You need have no worries. God is Almighty: He can hear everyone at the same time - and all the millions of others praying about the world at that moment!

It is also wise to be careful of using the word 'we'. Often you hear people pray, "Lord, we believe…" The person present has no idea what the others present believe. It is better to say, "I believe." The "Amen" by others is their agreement in faith: "It shall be so!"

**Wise leadership will give direction to a meeting, whether a small group or congregation, following the leading of the Holy Spirit, so that everyone can come into an agreement of faith.** Some need time to do this. Because the leader is in a place of faith, it does not mean that everyone else is in that same place of faith. It is a confused meeting if different people are believing for different things.

James says that a *"double-minded man"* is *"unstable in all he does." "That man should not think he will receive anything from the Lord."* *(James 1: 8,7)* The same thing could be said of a double-minded prayer meeting. Jesus tells us of the power of coming into an agreement of faith. A whole prayer meeting exercising such agreement is going to be exceedingly powerful, the Holy Spirit bearing witness with each believer as to what God will do in response to the prayer!

Both Jesus and the apostles cleared the room of unbelief before ministering healing to people. They knew the power of the agreement of faith. I am not suggesting that you clear the prayer meeting! However, it is better to address the unbelief, by suggesting that people ask the Lord for forgiveness of this lack of trust, and then it is good for the leader to open the Word to people's hearts, praying that the Holy Spirit will witness faith in every heart as he or she does so!

However, sometimes great sensitivity to the Spirit is needed by the leader, especially if praying about a situation where people's emotions are involved. If a brother or sister is near death and the meeting prays, everyone knows that God is able to perform a miracle. However, this is not always the outcome and the Spirit will make clear when this is the case. It is not helpful to lead a meeting in praising God for a healing that the Holy Spirit makes clear is not going to take place, even though the reasons for that outcome may not be clear! In such circumstances, it is best not to make grandiose claims about the outcome that people desire emotionally, but that God is not promising. **To go against the witness of the Spirit will only lead to confusion, disappointment and perplexity.** Again we see the importance of being led by the Spirit!

# 12

# DISTRACTIONS

We have seen that the flesh, the self-life, does not like to pray and resists the need to pray. Put simply: we often do not feel like praying!

Anyone who gives way to such negative feelings will never develop a satisfactory or powerful prayer life. **People of faith will not allow themselves to be governed by their feelings;** they will not allow their soul life to dominate their spirit, where Christ in them dwells by His Spirit. No, they will submit their souls - their minds, emotions and will - to be led and governed by the Spirit.

The result will be a disciplined prayer life. However, when we pray we can be subject to a number of distractions and we need to know how to deal with these.

## WANDERING THOUGHTS

This is the most widespread problem. It is annoying how easily you are able to concentrate on what you are doing, until you begin to pray. Suddenly, it seems, your mind wanders off onto all kinds of other things, many of them trivial. The enemy does not want you to pray. This is when he can be most active, not necessarily encouraging evil thoughts, but just distracting your concentration away from the Lord.

The best way to deal with wandering thoughts is not to allow yourself to become condemned for having them! That is exactly what the enemy wants you to think: that you are no good at praying, you cannot even concentrate; so you may as well go and do something else that will be more useful! Remember, he is the deceiver of the brethren and the father of lies. So don't take any notice of what he says!

**Self-concern can also cause wandering thoughts.** Instead of praying, you find yourself thinking about yourself, and worrying! The very opposite of faith! Again the enemy loves to encourage you to place yourself, instead of Jesus, at the centre of your prayer time, for he knows your prayer will then be ineffective.

Sometimes the believer is distracted by thoughts of sin and this causes him or her some distress. For example, he or she may have watched a movie with lurid or horrific scenes which come to mind as soon as he or she begins to pray.

This is not a distraction, but the Holy Spirit making it clear that God has no interest in your prayer until first you seek His forgiveness and the cleansing of His blood for the sin of watching such films that are offensive to Him. You will find that once you have sought the cleansing of the blood of Jesus, those images will recede and you can proceed to draw near to God's throne.

## EMOTIONS

It is far more difficult to pray objectively and to hear the voice of the Spirit clearly when we are praying about a situation in which we are involved emotionally. We can easily be confused as to what is of the Spirit and what is of our soulish emotions.

Again, do not allow yourself to be upset by this; it is understandable, and the Lord is well aware of this! It is best to pour out your heart and feelings to the Lord, thanking Him that He is much greater than your feelings! When hearing God, it is wise to check what we are hearing with others, sensitive to the Spirit, who are not involved in the situation emotionally. They can be more objective.

However, we will all make mistakes at times, and God does not condemn us for them. We all mistake the voice of emotion for the voice of God at times. The trouble is we say, "The Lord said to me…" when it is the voice of your own soul. If we say this often enough, we become convinced that it is really the voice of God we are hearing, and so become deceived. When things do not turn out as anticipated we are perplexed, saying: "The Lord said He was going to heal…" and the dear one has died.

The truth is that the Lord said no such thing, even though we wanted Him to! This is hard to accept because the emotions are involved. **If God had given such a promise, that would have been the outcome, for His word does not return to Him empty, but accomplishes the purpose for which it was sent!**

Again, although such situations are extremely difficult, it is better to acknowledge our own mistakes rather than blaming God for breaking a promise that never came from Him in the first place. In this we need to be humble, but not feel defeated.

It has been said that there are no mistakes in the Lord, except those we do not learn from! Do not allow such mistakes to prevent you from praying; that would only serve the enemy's purposes! Neither let them undermine your ability to hear God. Simply be wise, that when your emotions are deeply involved you find it difficult to discern clearly what God is saying just like everyone else!

# 13
# CONCLUSION

Much more could be said about all the prayer topics outlined in this short book. I refer you to other books I have written that deal with the subject much more fully. These will be of further help to you.

However, like playing a musical instrument, the only way to learn to pray is by doing it. I have never met anyone who claims to be good at praying. Everyone, it seems, is so aware of his or her shortcomings and knows that there is infinitely more of the Lord to know and discover in prayer. Right at the end of his life, after a very powerful and fruitful ministry, Paul said: *"I want to know Christ" (Philippians 3: 10)*. He understood that the more you know Him, the more there is to know of Him.

I believe we will need all eternity in heaven just to be able to appreciate and know Him fully! The wonderful truth is that when we see Him as He is, we shall be like Him. We shall take our place in that great host that praises Him eternally! And I guess that all the questions and inadequacies in prayer will be behind us! Alleluia!

However, I can testify to the truth that **the more you give of yourself to the Lord in prayer, the more rewarding your relationship with Him will become in this life. You will indeed reap what you sow!**

I thank God for a wonderful life of prayer that I have enjoyed with Him in over 50 years. During that time I have found the need, and the desire, to spend more and more time in prayer. In fact I often think now that it is by far the most valuable thing that I do! Praise God for His mercy and grace!

*Other books by Colin Urquhart and a catalogue of titles and teaching materials can be obtained from:*

Kingdom Faith Resources, Roffey Place, Old Crawley Road Faygate, Horsham, West Sussex RH12 4RU.
Telephone 01293 854 600 email: resources@kingdomfaith.com